Independent
Artist Guide

Greg 'Puntin' Cooks

DEDICATION

This book is dedicated to my beautiful children, Zealand and Journey. You two are a huge part of my "WHY."

CONTENTS

Introduction

1 Decide   Pg. #7

2 Know Your Why Pg. #11

3 Start   Pg. #15

4 Pre-production Pg. #20

5 Quality   Pg. #26

6 Networking   Pg. #30

7 Post-production Pg. #35

8 Music Business Pg. #40

9 Persistence   Pg. #46

10 Support System Pg. #51

INTRODUCTION

I was inspired to write this book in hopes that it will help independent artist around the world to achieve success in the music industry.

In understanding that there's different levels and perceptions of success, I want to first explain what success means to me. Success to me is doing what you truly love. You'd be surprised at how doing what you're passionate about can bring peace, harmony and joy into your life. Success is truly what you make it.

While goals are important and can indeed enhance your chances at success, what I believe to be even more important is your well-being. When pushing for your dreams and aspirations, things can grow to be stressful and disheartening if you're not careful. This is why I believe that one should pursue the dreams, hobbies and careers they absolutely love, rather than solely pursuing them for fame or notoriety.

Chapter 1

DECIDE

When deciding your position in the music industry, you must make a definite decision in-order to enhance your efficiency, effectiveness and level of success. Some people are built to be great managers, while others are built to be great artist. This is where I would personally advise to go with what you know. For example, go with your gut feeling. In choosing your profession in the music industry, it is vital that one chooses an area where they can blossom and sincerely be themselves.

There was one instance in the beginning of my career where a client suggested that I should perhaps stick to one profession rather than the two in which I saw myself pursuing.

He suggested that I should stick to producing and leave the rapping side of things alone. Boy, I am glad that I didn't listen to his impractical piece of advice. While I do understand what may have been his motive in trying to encourage me to mono-focus on the one thing that he thought I was better at, this dream was mine not his. Had I listened to him that day, I would have never toured overseas on six different occasions as I have. Trust me when I say that you and only you hold the key to your destiny. Again, go with what you know.

There is nothing wrong identifying with more than one profession. Just know and understand that more roles require more dedication. If you're confident that you can succeed in more than one music profession, then go for it.

I knew from the beginning that I was both a rapper and producer and no one could tell me different then and still can't tell me different now. I made my decision and here 20 plus years later, I am a successful rapper and producer. Decide exactly what you are, what you do, and what you want to accomplish.

Reflect:

- What is your profession in the music industry?

- Is your goal to be independent or signed, and why?

- What do you want to accomplish?

Chapter 2

KNOW YOUR WHY

Being a producer and engineer, I have worked with a countless number of artists over the years and I have realized that artist have different reasons why they have chosen to become a part of the music industry. For example, some artists pursue a career in the music industry because they want to become financially successful. Some do it for a hobby. Some do it to inspire others and some simply do it for the enjoyment of family and friends, while also for their own personal pleasure. I personally have no problem with either. I believe that you should do it for whatever reason you desire. Especially, if it provides you with personal peace and happiness.

However, I believe that it is vital to understand and know your "why."

In knowing your "why," you can better identify and focus on the necessary steps you need in-order to enhance your success. Know your audience, know your demographic, know your genre, know your market, know what you're willing to sacrifice, as well as what you're not willing to sacrifice. I discovered my "why" while living in my parents' home at the age of 17. My "why" was inspired by the title of a record label, World-wide Impact Records. A record label in which my mother and younger twin sisters were a part of. As I sat there staring at one of their cd covers that had a huge world on the center of it with bold words across the middle of the world saying "World-wide Impact." I was intrigued. It was at that moment that I realized I wanted my music to reach the world. In knowing this, I understood that my musical content could not be confined to just my region or nation, but instead it needed to be relatable to other parts of the world.

I then began to make music that had no boundaries. Music that a kid in London, England could relate to. Music that would encourage and inspire the world. Knowing and understanding these things helped me in discovering my "why." Another great and definitely most important part of my "why" are my two children, Zealand and Journey. They motivate me to strive for greatness no matter what things might look like.
At times its necessary to stop and ask yourself "where do you see yourself going in the music industry and why?" Once you've identified your "why," you can then aim straight at your target.

Reflect:

- Why have you chosen this profession?

- What is your demographic?

- Who is your audience?

- What is your genre?

- What are you willing and not willing to sacrifice to reach your desired success in this profession?

Chapter 3

START

In-order to reach a goal or finish a mission you must first start. We all know someone who constantly talks about all the grand things they're going to do, but never does any of it. You can have it all mapped out, know how you want to do it, when you want to do it, and even what it's going to take for you to do it. Yet, if you never start, it will never get done. Personally, I battle with procrastination. There are things that I know I can and should do; nonetheless, I have yet to start them.

We as artist have superpowers to create. We have been blessed with gifts, talents, ideas and the ability to turn blank canvases into creative masterpieces. As artist, we must understand that just starting alone gives us the competitive advantage over a great majority of inspiring artist.

There are millions of gifts, talents, ideas and dreams that never see the light of day. Whether it's because of procrastination, fear, doubt, or laziness, some people never utilize their superpowers. If you're one of these people, I challenge you on this day to start. Stop sleeping on yourself. I can understand the lack of others not recognizing your superpowers (gifts, talents and capabilities). However, what I can't understand is why you aren't using them. You would be surprised of what you could accomplish by simply starting. Starting could help you to overcome your procrastination in making a commitment to overcome your doubts and fears in facing them head on. Starting also displays faith by actively moving forward.

When you start you immediately minimize laziness by getting off your gluteus maximus and making things happen.

I believe that starting is one of the most important and essential keys to success. Not only is it critical that one sets goals and plans, but it is also vital that you start once those goals and plans are established. You can be the hottest in your city and have all the talent in the world; nevertheless, it's only potential until you make up in your mind to make it reality. Talk is cheap. A person can shout how good they are and how they will change the game, but if they never put any definite action behind that talk, they're simply just talking.

On another note, I never let the lack of finances keep me from starting. No matter the situation. Where there is a will, there is a way. When I thought that I couldn't afford a keyboard, I learned how to make beats on my PlayStation game console. When I thought that I couldn't afford to purchase studio time, I purchased studio equipment piece by piece until I had a complete recording studio.

I believe that excuses are like lies, no one wants to hear them. Rather than talking about it, be about it.

Reflect:

- Why is starting one of the most important and essential keys to success?

- What are some ways that artists can be effective without funding?

- Why does starting give artists a competitive edge?

Chapter 4

PRE-PRODUCTION

There's a famous saying that I've heard many of times throughout my career. "Music is 10% talent and 90% business." This ratio is what I believe to be the very reason that millions of talented artists never reach a certain level of success. Many artists have the talent and even the will to make it. However, the business side of things are obviously much more important when it comes to garnering success in the music industry. I recall being frustrated in pursuing to be discovered earlier on in my career. Rather than quitting or giving up like many artists do, I decided that I would purchase books about the music business and learn as much as I could on my own. In doing so, I was able to learn things such as budgeting, distribution, royalties, soundscan, encoding, marketing and much more. Because of this I have been able to reach heights that many independent artists seldom reach.

Success in the music industry as an independent artist requires learning and understanding what makes and breaks an artist. When I started out, things were completely different than they are today. Marketing and promotion consisted of my team and I being present in places that there were potential fans, while passing out promo cd's, posters and flyers. Back in the day you were only as good as your street team. Today, things are mostly virtual and digital. Nowadays, you can truly say an artist is only as good as their social media presence. With TikTok, YouTube, Instagram, Facebook and many more social media platforms, there is undeniably more opportunity for an artist to breakout. Artist today can go viral and become overnight sensations. It can be said that the music industry market is flooded and oversaturated due to everyone and their momma being able to utilize the internet. The digital age has far more benefits now than when I started in the early 2000s.

When it comes to pre-production, there are key things that an artist should keep in mind, such as budgeting, presentation and vision. An artist should always understand what their budget is before starting a new project. For example, if your budget is $5000, you should create a spreadsheet or a record keeping system that itemizes the different expenses in-order to successfully complete and release the project. Many artists never figure this part out and have to pay the consequences. Either they never complete the project or expend their budget in the production process which then leaves them nothing to market and promote it. A lot of artist simply spend their budget on everything other than their project. You know, like on expensive designer shoes and clothes, custom jewelry, drugs and so on. Don't get me wrong, I am not indifferent to looking good and feeling good. However, if it's going to hinder the success of my project and career, sticking with the "Jones'" can wait.

Over the years I've come across many talented artists who just don't get it. Success in the music business takes true dedication and discipline and without it, you put yourself and career at a huge disadvantage. Pre-production is one of the most important steps in attaining a successful career in the music industry. Before one single song is produced, one should have a clear understanding of their budget and vision for that song/project.

In a nutshell, learn and understand project management or hire someone to manage your projects for you until you do.

Reflect:

- Why is project budgeting important?

- Why is project management important?

- Why is presentation and vision important?

Chapter 5

QUALITY

Finding your sound is critical to your success in the music industry. One can be super gifted and talented, but if their production and sound is not good it can hinder them tremendously. Finding the right producer(s) and engineer(s) can be difficult, but it is major that you do. I know people who won't give your song 20 seconds of play if the beat isn't to their liking. As far as sound quality, there's no legit radio station that I know of playing a song with bad sounding quality. They know and understand that if they play music that sounds bad, not only will their ratings drop, but their jobs could be on the line as well. This is why it is significant to find good sound production that will enhance your sound rather encumber it. I understand that independent artists don't have the same budget as artists on major record labels. However, there are countless numbers of producers and engineers available on social media, as well as platforms such as Beat Stars and Air Bit. Oh yeah, let's not forget, ya boy Puntin. One of the best producers to ever do it. If I do say so myself. I'm a genius with the keys. Always cooking up top quality beats. I know Pookie up the street records and sells beats for $15, but please don't cheat yourself being cheap. Holla at me.

When it comes to first impression and presentation, an artist's quality of graphics and packaging also plays an immense role in their level of success. For example, if an artist's graphic art and packaging is exceptional, it gives them a fighting chance to be taken seriously. Trust me when I say that consumers pay close attention to these things. You can literally give someone your cd for free, but if the graphic art and packaging is atrocious, they won't even bother taking it out of the plastic shrink-wrap. Let alone listen to it. They may feel that if you're not dedicated enough to take your time and present something that looks professional, you're most likely not dedicated enough to take your time to create a professional sound. Again, there are countless numbers of graphic artist and producers available online for artist to utilize and obtain professional quality. So please don't cheat yourself being cheap.

Reflect:

- Why are quality graphics important?

- Why is quality sound production important?

- How can first impression and presentation impact the level of one's success?

Chapter 6

NETWORKING

My music career began when I started playing the drums for my mother and sisters gospel group, "Gloria, Twynz & Friend." I traveled weekend after weekend throughout Texas and the southern region playing drums at different Church's, auditoriums, conferences and festivals. For six years straight, I did so and met many great music industry shakers, musicians, radio announcers and music lovers. I didn't know it then, but today I realize that I was building up a pleasant network. Those same people were beneficial in the success that I accumulated years later as rapper and producer. Unlike most who start their music careers from ground zero, when I began rapping, I already had a network of individuals, radio announcers, promotors and organizations who were eagerly ready to book me on their calendars. This shows the importance of networking.

I highly recommend that artist should get out and go to conferences, music seminars, network gatherings, etc. These are the same individuals who can assist you in reaching your goals. Exchange numbers and build relationships. I still communicate with individuals in the music industry who I met when I was 12 years old. Now that we're in the digital age, we have access to network with people all over the world via the web. It's key that as artist we utilize all the tools that we have at our fingertips today. In the earlier part of my rapping career, I utilized Myspace to form an organization called King Christ Movement. After networking and meeting different rappers from different states and countries, the vision came to me when looking at my top friends list. I realized that my top friends list consisted of all the rappers I had met and networked with from Myspace. I figured that if I could get all of us on one accord and form a movement that we all embraced and shared as one, it could be massive. Not only did 40 different rappers agree to join and be a part of the movement, we eventually ended up releasing a compilation album and going on tour together. The power of networking is limitless. I could go on and on for days about the great connections I've made by networking over the years. Don't just sit behind your mobile device or computer keyboards, get out and rub shoulders. You never know where it could take you and your career. For example, I met my good friend and fellow artist, BossTon through a mutual friend/client at a studio session. We then began to recognize each other outside the studio until one day finally exchanging numbers and connecting. Thanks to this network, BossTon and I have gone on to perform on six world tours together. I met my good friend and southern legend, E.S.G. backstage at a concert where my rap group and I had opened up for him. I informed him that I was a producer and we exchanged information. Not even a month later I produced a song of his titled "Hold Up" that would go on to get airtime on one of Houston's biggest radio stations, 97.9 the Box. Just to think, this all came to pass because of networking.

Reflect:

- Why is networking important?

- How can you improve your current network?

Chapter 7

Post-Production

This is the step where a lot of artist struggle. After the project is complete and ready to be released to the world, many artists have no earthly idea on what to do. I've witnessed artist spend enormous amounts of money on beats, features, studio time, presentation and packaging just to get to this point and drop the ball. Post-production also falls into the "music is 90% business and 10% talent" category. This is an area where artists must launch campaigns, promote, market and sell themselves. An artist must know who their audience is, where their audience is, and how they're going to get the word out to their audience successfully. It troubles me to see an artist put so much effort, money and time into a project just to post a flyer and link on their social media platform one-time telling people to go check it out. Now I know that there's big name artists who can successfully release albums out the blue and break the internet, but most independent artists don't possess the multitude of followings to successfully do so. The independent artist must be strategic and strategize a well and thought-out marketing plan. For example, I consider it a no-brainer that independent artists should make their project available for pre-order at-least 1-3 weeks prior to its release date. This gives the artist leverage to accumulate as many units pushed as they can before the project's official release date. This not only gives the artist time to promote and market what they have coming, but it also helps their chances of charting being that pre-order sells will be included in their first week sells. Let's just say that you're an artist releasing an album and you've promoted and marketed your pre-orders well enough that you've accumulated 500 units sold. This increases your chances extremely high, rather than meekly posting it on social media out the blue with no promo or heads up.

When consulting for artists, I inform them that pre-orders, music videos, sponsored ads, and friendly challenges to get their audiences involved can exceedingly boost their chances at successfully releasing a project. Be creative. Do whatever it takes to catch your audiences' attention and make them aware of your project. Many artists aren't aware of these types of things. They just make the music and hope that the world latches on. However, that's a recipe for disaster in an industry where millions and millions of artists around the world are striving to breakthrough. It's more than just making music; you really have to put in the extra energy if you want to stand out from the rest. When I began producing, I pondered for days on a creative way to get the word out. Then ding. I got it. I would contact every artist I knew and present them with a deal they couldn't deny. I would produce and give them a beat that they could use for themselves. Yet, I could also use the song they recorded on my beat for a project that I would release called "Street Bangers." It worked! Every music lover in my city and surrounding cities now knew I was a producer with hot beats. Not only did they know, but the artists who were on the tape, and several other artists knew that had hot beats as well.

Reflect:

- How can pre-orders help independent artists?

- Why are project campaigns important?

- Why do independent artists struggle in successfully releasing projects?

- What are some creative strategies that artists can utilize to grow their market?

Chapter 8

THE MUSIC BUSINESS

Here's where all the books I've read about the music business helped out. Learning about the different types of royalties, how to register your project for SoundScan, encoding, etc. When I started years ago there wasn't as many outlets for independent artists like there is now. If you weren't on a record label back then, you were pretty much pushing and selling your cd's out of the trunk. Today, there's several platforms where independent artists can release and distribute their music on iTunes, Amazon, Spotify, Tidal and YouTube alongside the "big dawgs." With a large enough following I would even suggest that going the independent route could be more lucrative and worry-free. Let's use this scenario: An artist has an account of 100k active followers which helps them in averaging 5,000k-10,000k units sold at $10 per project. This means that the artist is averaging $50,000-$100,000 and making more than the average American household income from one project. That's not considering what the artist can accumulate from streams, concerts, tours, and merchandise. With the proper approach, a successful music career isn't as far-fetched as many assume.

I speak with artists about the business side of things all of the time to only discover that they have no idea what Nielsen SoundScan, MediaBase, Songtrust, Music Reports, SoundExchange, ASCAP and BMI are. They're basically leaving money on the table if they're not associated with these companies. These sources are fundamental in an independent artists success.

Back in 2011 I released a project titled, Reversing the Curse. Independently, I would say the album did great. I suddenly began receiving calls from promoters in various states following this particular release. It then dawned on me that I could probably coordinate my own tour by creating a flyer that displayed the shows that I had already booked and added "Now Booking" with my contact information for booking inquiries. I ended up doing just that and booked my first national tour that consisted of me touring and performing in places such as Seattle, Washington; Pueblo, Colorado; Baltimore, Maryland; Boise, Idaho; and several cities in Texas. I had coordinated my first national tour by simply creating a flyer and communicating via phone and e-mail to conduct particulars. I would seriously recommend that musicians learn as much about the music business as they can even if their goals and desires aren't to pursue an independent career. Trust me, I get it. Some artist would prefer to do without the added responsibilities and duties of handling the business side of things. They would rather focus on the music and the music alone. I completely understand and quite frankly agree that it's probably better to have someone in position who's knowledgeable to handle the business while they focus on making great music. I recommend that artist learn about the music business as much as they can in-order to help prevent from possibly getting screwed over. While the music industry is an awesome and respected industry that has propelled many to fame and riches, it would be dishonest of me not to speak on the ugly side of it. I'm sure you've heard of the various stories about artists being screwed over in bogus deals. Hey, I've personally experienced a bogus deal myself. I once signed a national distribution deal that on a good note landed one of my projects in Walmart, Target, Best Buy and Barnes & Noble's. And on a bad note, let's just say I never got paid. I learned my lesson. Having your business intact can prevent you from these types of situations. Now that I have a better understanding of the music business, I can conduct my own tours, release my own projects and collect my own royalties. If ever I sign with a record label or a distribution company in the future, I'm prepared to make sure that all my i's are dotted, and my t's are crossed.

Reflect:

- Why is it important that artists learn about the music business?

- Why should artists be familiar be with Nielsen SoundScan, MediaBase, Songtrust, Music Reports, SoundExchange, ASCAP and BMI?

Chapter 9

Persistence

Longevity in the music industry is not an easy task to conquer. In my 20 plus year venture in this business I have seen many come and go. If there's one thing that I would tell someone who's inspiring to be an artist, it is that you must be persistent. Besides the few artists who somehow blew up overnight, most successful careers took years to flourish and develop. I've heard numerous stories from some of my favorite artists explaining how they had to grind for a great number of years before finally catching their big break. There may be times when you as an artist want to give up due to the lack of support from friends and family. Or simply because you may feel that accomplishing your goals in the music industry is too far-fetched. Those who make it in this industry are those who have the will power and endurance to overcome all test and obstacles that arise. There have been times throughout my career where I felt that no one believed in me an as artist. It hurts even worse when you feel that your family and people who you consider your loved ones don't believe in you. However, in-order to continue moving forward and past those instances I had to fully believe in myself. I had to make up in my mind that if no one believed in Puntin as an artist, Puntin believing in himself was more than enough. An additional area that I've found it hard for many artists to sustain throughout my career is how to stay consistent and current as the sound and style of music changes. I have witnessed artists who once made great music in the earlier part of my career get left behind in time because they couldn't adapt or refused to adapt and evolve with the emergent of music. When music changes, artists must change with it. I am not saying that artists should change their entire style or content. However, if an artist's goal is stay current in today's time of music it is crucial that they adapt with the current sound of music. This could consist of them having to adjust their style of music production, audio recording and mixing, vocal arrangement and more. If your goal is to stay current, be willing to change and adjust. Personally, I recall disliking the whole auto-tune phase when it seemed that every rapper resorted to using it on every song. Nevertheless, I found myself utilizing it in a few albums of my own. Same with 808 beats. Many fellow producers of mine were determined to stay away from the 808-beat phase and surprisingly found their selves stuck in the past. Not me, I got right on in where I fit in and found myself utilizing 808 beats to produce for other artists, as well as in a few albums of my own. I understand that music will continue to change with time and therefore, I must understand that change is inevitable if I want to remain a name in the game.

REFLECT:

- Why is it important for artists to be persistent?

- How does an artist maintain persistence?

- Why is it important for an artist to change, adjust and adapt with music?

Chapter 10

Support System

A support system plays a grand role in the success of an artist's career. A support system can either make or break an artist. An artist can be talented and gifted with undeniable potential, but if they do not have any support to back that up they can easily go unseen and unheard. I highly recommend that new and inspiring artists should record, and share covers and remixes of popular and current hit songs. I believe that this is one of the most effective and efficient strategies in growing a fanbase and support system. I've noticed that listeners tend to click on covers and remixes of hit songs before they click on new songs by new and undiscovered artists. I utilized this strategy a great deal when starting out. I recorded entire mixtapes using instrumentals from current and popular hit songs. Not only did I capture thousands of subscribers, fans and views on YouTube, but I also garnered thousands of streams and downloads on various mixtape platforms. Back when I started out, A&R's and record labels scoped-out and recruited artists based off of pure talent. Today, pure talent will likely only get you so far. A&R's and record labels are now searching for artists who have established active and substantial fanbases. Rather than discovering talent that they have to prep and build new fanbases for, they now take the easier route in discovering talent that's already polished, ready to go and artist who only needs some push to get them over the top. This further expresses the importance of a significant social media presence. Today, it is critical that artists find ways to create a presence on the internet if they want to be discovered. Those days of knocking on record label doors and blowing them away with pure talent and demo tapes are pretty much distinct. We as artist today have to be creative, different and unique. We must always try to figure out ways that we can standout from the rest, as well as ways to connect and tap-in with the millions of potential fans online and around the world.

REFLECT:

- Why does a support system play such a huge role in the success of an artist's career?

- What are some ways that artists can grow their fanbase/support system?

- Why is a social media presence important?

Resources:

U.S. Copyright Office

Performing arts registry.

Ascap

Membership association for songwriters, composers and music publishers.

DistroKid

Independent music distribution service.

Nielsen SoundScan

Title registry.

SoundExchange

Digital performance rights collector.

Acknowledgements

Thanks to everyone who has played a role in my musical journey. Especially my parents, Johnnie and Gloria Cooks for instilling persistence inside of me at a young age. I owe many thanks to my lovely wife, Victoria Cooks, for all of her help, encouragement and support. Thanks to my family, friends and supporters who have continued to support me throughout my musical career. Thanks to God for blessing me with the talent, vision and health to pursue my dreams.

About the Author

Greg 'Puntin' Cooks is an international hip-hop artist, producer, and speaker who has helped a countless number of people transform their personal and spiritual lives via his music, concerts, conferences and products. He is an alumnus of the University of Phoenix, where he received his Bachelor of Science in Business degree and his Master of Management degree.

Made in the USA
Middletown, DE
11 September 2022